CONTENTS

LET'S LOOK AT THE SKY:
THE PLANETS

The name of Patrick Moore is
synonymous with night skies,
constellations, Apollo Moon shots, and
BBC radio and television broadcasting.

In LET'S LOOK AT THE SKY:
THE PLANETS Patrick Moore covers
such topics as The Earth in Space;
How the Moon moves; When the Sun
is hidden; Mars, the Red Planet; the
Moons of Jupiter and Shooting Stars.
This book is profusely illustrated with
'easy-to-follow' diagrams and there are
lots of experiments for you to do as you
discover an absorbing new world.

Also by Patrick Moore

THE ASTRONOMY QUIZ BOOK
LET'S LOOK AT THE SKY: THE STARS

and published by CAROUSEL BOOKS

Patrick Moore

LET'S LOOK AT
THE SKY:
THE PLANETS

Illustrated by Lawrence Clarke
and Jocelyn Knox

Consultant editor: Anne Wood

TRANSWORLD PUBLISHERS LTD

LET'S LOOK AT THE SKY: THE PLANETS

A CAROUSEL BOOK 0 552 54081 1
First published in Great Britain 1975

PRINTING HISTORY
Carousel edition published 1975

Carousel books are published by Transworld
Publishers Ltd.,
Cavendish House, 57–59 Uxbridge Road,
Ealing, London, W.5.

Made and printed in Great Britain by
Cox & Wyman Ltd., London, Reading and Fakenham

EARTH AND SKY

WHEN you look up into a clear sky during the day, you see the Sun. The sky is blue, and the Sun is so bright that if you look straight at it you will hurt your eyes. After the Sun has set, and the sky has become dark, the stars come out. There are also some objects which look like stars, but which are very different. We call them *planets*, and we live on one planet: our own Earth.

The science of the Sun, the Moon, the stars and everything else in the sky is called *astronomy*, and the people who study it are called *astronomers*. In this book and *Let's Look At The Sky: The Stars* I want to tell you as much about astronomy as I can – and also show you how to start taking a real interest in it.

Have you ever thought about the size and shape of the Earth? People who lived long ago thought that the world must be flat, and they also thought that it stayed quite still, with the sky moving round it once in 24 hours. Then it was found that the Earth is not flat at all; it is shaped like a big ball, and it is spinning round. It is this spinning of the Earth which makes the sky seem to move.

You can show this by standing up in the middle of a room and turning very quickly round and round. You will soon become giddy, and the room will seem to be moving round you – because you are spinning. If the

Earth did not spin, the sky would not seem to move.

The Sun is a star. This may sound surprising, but it is true. Many of the stars you can see at night are much larger and hotter than the Sun. They are made up of gas, and they are shining because they are so hot. Each star is a sun; the stars look fainter than our Sun only because they are so much further away from us.

Even our Sun is very distant. It is 150 million kilometres from the Earth. Suppose you could fly from the Earth to the Sun, travelling at a speed of 1600 kilometres an hour and never stopping at all; how long would it take you? The journey to the Sun would last for over ten years. Of course, nobody could ever fly to the Sun, but space-travellers have at least been to the Moon, which is much closer to us and is made up of rock in the same way as the Earth.

The Earth goes round the Sun, and the Moon goes round the Earth. The Moon is much smaller than the Earth, and it has no light of its own. It shines because it is being lit up by the Sun, just as you can light up a tennis-ball in a dark room by shining a torch on it. If for any reason the Sun suddenly stopped shining, the Moon would disappear too.

I have said that the Earth is a planet. It is not the only one; in the Sun's family or Solar System there are eight other planets, some of them bigger than the Earth and others smaller. Like the Moon, they shine because they are being lit up by the Sun.

Though the Earth and the other planets move round the Sun, the stars do not. Many of the stars may have planet-families of their own, though we cannot be sure.

The Sun's light comes to us through the air around the Earth. The air spreads the sunlight around, and makes the sky blue. The reason why we cannot see stars in the daytime is that the sky is too bright; the stars are there all the time, but they do not come into view until after the Sun has set.

THE EARTH IN SPACE

THE Earth spins round and round, making one turn every 24 hours. This is why we have our day and night. Of course, the Sun can light up only half the Earth at any one time, so that half the Earth is in daylight while the other half is having its night. Because the Earth spins, each part of its surface is carried from the daylight to the night side, and then back again.

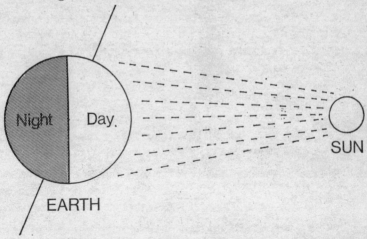

The picture here shows the Earth, with its north pole and its south pole. The line running through both poles and the middle of the Earth is called the *axis*, and the Earth spins on this axis. A good way to make a model is to push a stick through a soft ball (a ball of wool will do quite well) and then spin the ball round. Do this in a dark room, using a torch to shine on the ball, and you will see that each part of the ball will be first in the light and then in darkness.

Because the Earth takes about 24 hours to make one turn, each 'day' is about 12 hours long (because 12 is half of 24) and each 'night' is also about 12 hours long, although, as we all know, the daylight periods are rather longer in the summer than in the winter. This is because the Earth is tipped over as it moves round the Sun, and we have our seasons of spring, summer, autumn and winter.

The Earth goes round the Sun in a path which is very nearly a circle, but not quite. It is strange to find that the Earth is at its closest to the Sun in December, when it is winter in England and snow covers the ground. In June we are further away from the Sun, though the difference is not really very great.

The Earth's axis, on which it spins, is tilted over as shown in the picture. In June, the north pole is tipped towards the Sun, and countries such as England are having the best of the sunlight. In December it is the south pole which is tipped towards the Sun, and the north pole is tipped away – so that it is summer in countries such as Australia, but winter in England and the United States.

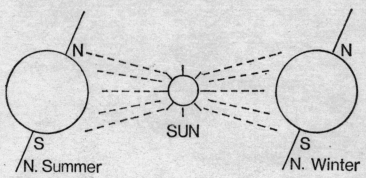

N. Summer   N. Winter

There is something else which can be seen from the picture. In June, the Sun's rays are falling on to the north pole all the time, so that there is no night at all but the light from the Sun can never reach the south pole, because the bulge of the Earth gets in the way. This means that each 'day' and each 'night' at the Earth's poles lasts for half a year, or six months.

Further away from the poles, the Sun rises and sets with each turn of the Earth, but the difference in the length of the day is very easy to notice. In North Scotland the days in summer are much longer than they are in London; but in winter the days in North Scotland are much shorter than in London, while the nights are both longer and colder.

The Earth is divided into two parts by its equator. To

show what this means, take an orange, and use a knife to cut it into two equal parts, as the boy in the picture is doing. If you then put the two parts together again, the line where the knife has made its cut will be in the position of the orange's equator. Great Britain and the United States of America lie in the northern part of the Earth, while Australia and New Zealand are in the southern part.

To anyone living in the northern part of the Earth, the Sun will be due south at mid-day, and of course it will be higher in the sky during summer than during winter. You can follow this quite easily if you put a stick up on your lawn, and measure the length of the shadow at mid-day. In summer, the shadow will be shorter than it is in winter.

All of us feel heavy because of what is called the force of gravity. The Earth is very massive, and it tries to pull everything down towards its centre. If you pick up a book and then let it go, the book will fall, because the Earth is pulling it down. Nobody really knows what gravity is; but all the bodies in the sky have it, and, indeed, so have you and I. The more massive the body, the greater is its pull of gravity, so that the Moon, which is not nearly so massive as the Earth, pulls less strongly. (The 'mass' of a body is not the same thing as the 'weight'; if you could go to the Moon you would find that you weighed much less than you do on Earth, though your mass would be the same as before.)

If you look at a drawing of the Earth, you will see that England and Australia are on opposite sides. In the top picture given on page 16, it looks as though England is on the top and Australia on the bottom. But there is no true 'top' or 'bottom' in space, and there is no reason why we should not draw the Earth with Australia towards the top, as in the picture below.

We have seen that the Earth is a planet. We live on its surface, which is solid and rocky. The Earth is not like

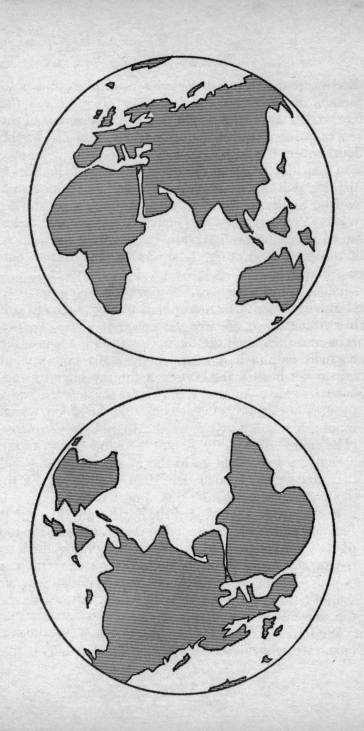

this all the way through its globe, and its inside is hot, though not nearly as hot as that of the Sun. Unfortunately we cannot dig down for more than a very few kilometres, and even now we are not sure just what the centre of the Earth is like. At a depth of only a few kilometres rocks are so hot that they are melted – and there is no chance of our being able to bore a hole through the Earth from England to Australia!

The Earth has air round it. If there were no air, there would be nothing for us to breathe, and there could be no life here. Yet the air does not stretch upward for very far. Men who have climbed to the top of Everest, the highest mountain in the world, have had to take special masks with them, because at that height the air is too thin to breathe. Everest is less than 8 kilometres high, and at a greater height the air is thinner still. Above 300 or 400 kilometres there is almost no air left, and there is none at all in the space between the Earth and the Moon.

The Earth is the only planet in the Sun's family to have air of this kind, and so it is the only planet upon which we could live. Also, the Earth is the only world with seas on its surface. The other planets are quite different, as we will see later in this book.

3

THE ASTRONOMER
AND HIS TELESCOPES

WHEN you look up into the night sky, you will see the stars as points of light. The planets will look much the same, though some of them are brighter than any of the stars. If you want to see very faint stars, or if you want to see markings on the planets, you must use something more powerful than your eyes.

Astronomers use telescopes, which make distant objects appear closer, and which can pick up light which is too faint to be seen with the eye alone. The bigger the telescope, the more it will show you. The biggest telescope in the world is so large that the astronomer using it can sit inside it!

Telescopes are of two kinds. Some of them collect their light by using pieces of glass called *lenses*; others collect their light by means of special mirrors. Let us first look at lens telescopes, which are known as *refractors*.

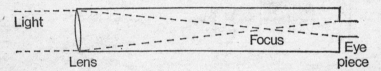

Light

Focus

Eye
piece

Lens

The diagram here shows how a refractor works. The light from the Moon, or whatever you are looking at, passes through the glass lens at the top of the telescope, which is called the object-glass. This lens bunches the rays of light up, and makes them meet near the bottom of the telescope tube. At this point, called the focus, an image of the Moon is formed. The image is then made larger by another lens, which is really a special kind of

magnifying glass; astronomers call it an eyepiece. When using the telescope, you look up the tube, as the girl in the picture is doing.

All the small telescopes used by people who want to watch birds, or to look at ships out to sea, are of this kind; but there is one thing to notice. An astronomer's telescope turns everything upside-down. In fact, all telescopes will do this, but with a telescope meant for use on land there is an extra lens to turn the picture the right way up again. (Otherwise, the telescope would be very difficult to use.) Astronomers do not mind the Moon or a planet being shown upside-down, and every time a new lens is put into the tube a little light is lost, which is something that the astronomer does not want at all. He needs to collect all the light that he can.

In your house there may well be a pair of binoculars. The ordinary pair of binoculars is made up of two small telescopes joined together, so that you can use both your eyes at the same time instead of only one. Of course, you can hold the binoculars easily in your hand. An astronomer's telescope, which has bigger lenses, is too heavy to be hand-held, and you must have a stand for it.

The power of a telescope can be changed by using different eyepieces. A strong magnifying-glass will give you a bigger picture than a weak one, but it will also mean that you must be even more cafeful to keep the telescope really steady, which is why it is so important to have the telescope on a firm stand. Also, making the image larger also makes it fainter; and if you try to use too strong an eyepiece, the picture will be too faint to be seen at all.

The second kind of telescope uses a mirror to collect its light, and is called a *reflector*. Here, the light goes down an open tube until it hits the mirror at the bottom. The mirror is not flat; it is curved, and it reflects the light back up the tube, bunching the rays together. The light then hits a second mirror, which is smaller and which

really is flat. The rays are sent to the side of the tube, and
this is where we put our eyepiece or magnifying-glass.
With a telescope of this sort, you have to look 'into' the
tube instead of 'up' it. This may seem awkward, but one
soon becomes used to it.

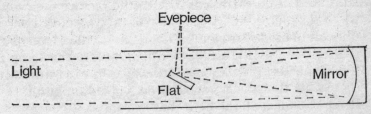

There are several different kinds of reflectors, but all
of them work by using mirrors. A piece of ordinary glass,
or even a looking-glass, will not do. The mirror has to be
specially shaped, and then a thin layer of something
such as silver is put over it to make it reflect as much
light as possible.

Of course, a reflector must have a very firm stand. To
help in pointing the telescope in the right direction, a
much smaller telescope can be fixed to the side of the
tube, as shown here; this is called a *finder*, because it
helps you to find things. First, put the Moon (or whatever you want to see) in the middle of the field of view of
the finder. If the finder is properly set up, you will then
see the Moon as soon as you look into the eyepiece of the
big telescope.

The finder itself is almost always a lens telescope or
refractor, and, of course, an astronomer's refractor can
also have a finder of the same kind.

The size of a telescope is measured not by its length,
but by the size of its lens (for a refractor) or its main
mirror (for a reflector). If the lens of a refractor is 7.5
cm across, we say that the telescope is a *7.5 cm refractor*,

4

HOW THE MOON MOVES

THE Moon is our companion in space. It stays with us as we go round the Sun, and it is much closer than anything else in the sky. This is why it looks so bright. It is not as big as the Earth, as you can see from the picture; if you make a model in which the Earth is the size of a tennis-ball, the Moon will be no larger than a table-tennis ball.

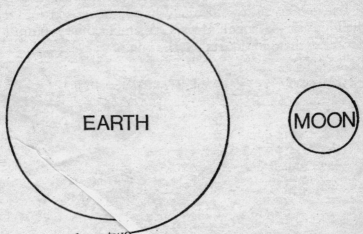

Using these two you can show how far away the Moon is. Take a pie string, and wrap it round the tennis-ball ten times. I wind the string and pull it tight. Put the table-tennis the other end of it, and you will have your model Earth and Moon at about the right distance apart.

It used to be thought that the Moon was once part of the Earth, and that it broke away before the Earth had become solid. We now know that this is not true. The Moon has always been a separate body. It is about the same age as the Earth, and must have been born in the same way. We believe that the Earth, the Moon and the planets were formed out of a cloud of dust and gas which used to go round the Sun.

The Moon seems to change its shape. Sometimes it is full, sometimes half, sometimes shaped like a crescent –

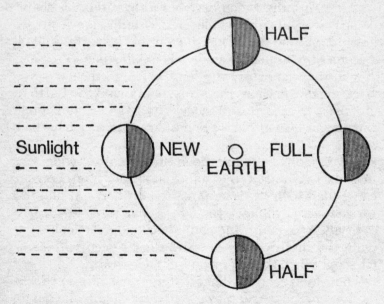

and sometimes it cannot be seen at all. Of course, the Moon is not really changing its shape. Like the planets, it has no light of its own, and it shines only because it is being lit up by the Sun. Only half of it can shine at any

water-heaps do not turn with it. They stay under the Moon, so that each place on Earth should have two high tides and two low tides every day.

Things are not really so simple as this, and the different shapes of the lands and oceans make the tides less regular than they would otherwise be. The Sun also causes tides; but these are not so strong as the tides due to the Moon, because the Sun is so much further away from us. When the Sun and the Moon are pulling together, we have strong tides, as happens when the Moon is new or full (so that the Sun, the Earth and the Moon are more or less in a line). When the Moon is at half, it is pulling against the Sun, and the tides are weaker. The weak tides are called *neap tides*; the strong tides are called *spring tides*, though they have nothing to do with the season of spring.

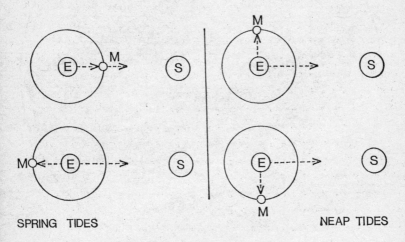

SPRING TIDES   NEAP TIDES

ings. The Moon is a world of grey plains, high mountains, deep valleys, and circular, walled craters. There is
no air, and so there can be no clouds to hide the surface
from us.

The grey patches on the Moon are always called *seas*,
because when men first looked at the Moon through
telescopes they thought that the patches were caused by
water. This is not true; with no air, there can be no
water. The Moon is quite dry, and it is not likely that
there have ever been seas there, but we still use the old
names.

There are high mountains on the Moon, some of
which are named after mountains on the Earth. The
Apennines of the Moon are easy to find, particularly
when the Moon is just over half-full. The Apennines run
round the edge of one of the grey plains which we call
the Sea of Rains. Another mountain range, also on the
edge of this sea, is called the Alps. A great valley, 129
kilometres long, cuts through the Alps.

There are many craters on the Moon. These are
walled holes, with floors which are sunk deeply below
the outside country, and with walls which reach up to
thousands of metres above the crater-bottoms. Some of
the craters have mountains inside them, while others
have floors which look flat.

A crater is best seen when it is near the edge of the
Moon's sunlit part, because there will be shadows inside
it, thrown by the walls across the floor. The pictures here
show the same crater as it looks at three different times.
The crater is called *Ptolemæus* (pronounced 'tolly-may-
us'), and it is over 150 kilometres across, so that it could
stretch across England all the way between Brighton and
Cambridge. At about half-moon, when the Sun is rising
over Ptolemæus, the crater has black shadow on its floor.

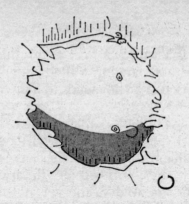
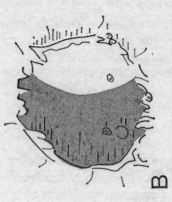
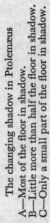

The changing shadow in Ptolemæus

A—Most of the floor in shadow.
B—Little more than half the floor in shadow.
C—Only a small part of the floor in shadow.

Later, when the Moon is near full, there is much less shadow; and at the time of full moon there is no shadow at all, so that the crater is hard to find even when you know just where to look for it.

In fact, full moon is the very worst time to start trying to learn which crater is which. Also, there are some craters from which come bright streaks or rays, crossing the Moon and hiding the craters and mountains. The best-known of these ray-craters is called *Tycho*; it lies in the south part of the Moon, and rays from it spread out for hundreds of kilometres in all directions.

The Tycho rays

If you look at the full moon with binoculars you will find Tycho easily, near the bottom of the Moon's face. In the picture I have shown Tycho near the top – because, as you will remember, an astronomer's telescope turns everything upside-down.

Most of the big craters are round, but some of them have been broken into by smaller craters, so that they are not regular in shape. This seems to show that some of the craters are older than others. It is useful to make models of craters, using sand; if you do this, and then shine a torch from the side in a darkened room, you will see that the walls cast shadows. As you move the torch up and down, the shadows will alter, just as happens on the Moon.

How did the Moon get its craters? We cannot yet be sure. Some astronomers think that the large craters were made by pieces of rock coming from space and hitting the Moon; if you throw a pebble into your sand model, it will make a hole. Other astronomers think that the craters are volcanic. We have volcanoes on the Earth, and we have craters too, though the craters are not so big as those of the Moon. Very probably there are craters of both kinds on the Moon.

One thing you will notice, as soon as you look at the Moon, is that there are no bright colours. The surface looks yellowish-grey everywhere, with black shadows. The shadows are very black indeed, because there is no air on the Moon to spread the sunlight about.

If you want to learn your way around the Moon, take a simple map and then, using your telescope (or binoculars) start finding the craters and mountains which are shown on the map. The craters are named after famous people of the past. For example, Ptolemæus was a great astronomer who lived two thousand years ago, while Tycho was a Danish astronomer who died in the year that Elizabeth I became Queen of England.

6

ECLIPSES OF THE MOON

IF you light up a ball in a darkened room, the ball will cast a shadow. The Earth, too, casts a shadow in space. Sometimes the Moon passes into this shadow, so that the sunlight can no longer reach it. This causes what we call a *lunar eclipse,* or eclipse of the Moon.

The position during an eclipse is shown in the diagram. The Earth blocks out the sunlight; and since the Moon shines only by reflecting the rays of the Sun, it becomes very dim. It does not disappear, because the Earth has air round it, and some of the Sun's rays are bent when they pass through the air, so that they really do reach the Moon. In the diagram, these bent rays are shown as dotted lines. If the Earth had no air, there would be nothing to bend the sunlight on to the Moon, and the Moon would vanish completely during an eclipse.

An eclipse may be either total, when all the Moon goes into the Earth's shadow, or partial, when not all the Moon is covered. An eclipse may be total for over an hour.

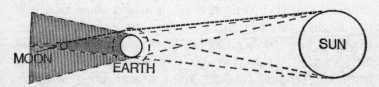

As you will see from the picture, an eclipse of the Moon can happen only when the Moon is full. The Sun, the Earth and the Moon must be in a line, with the Earth in the middle position – and this, of course, means that the Moon must have all its sunlight half turned towards us.

Why do we not have an eclipse at every full moon? The reason is that the Moon's path round the Earth is tipped, rather in the way that two hoops may be tipped to each other as shown in the next drawing. This means that at most full moons, the Moon is not quite in line

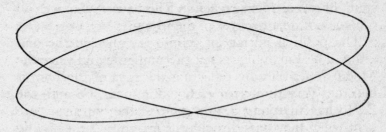

with the Sun and the Earth; it is either above or below the Earth's shadow, and so it does not go into eclipse. Usually, there are at least two eclipses of the Moon every year, though not all of them are visible from England.

During an eclipse, the Moon often looks coppery in colour. If you have a telescope, or binoculars, you will be able to see this colour well, and the sight is really beautiful.

People who lived long ago did not know the cause of eclipses, and they were often frightened when they saw the Moon losing its light. There is a story about the great explorer Christopher Columbus, who was in the island of Jamaica in the year 1504 and wanted the natives there to give him food for himself and the crew of his ship. The natives were not friendly, and said that they would not give him anything. Columbus knew that there would be an eclipse that night, so he told the natives that he would make the Moon 'go out'. When the eclipse started, the natives were so frightened that they quickly gave Columbus all the food that he wanted!

7

THE OTHER SIDE OF THE MOON

WHENEVER you look at the Moon, the 'seas', the mountains and the craters are always seen in the same places. The ray-crater Tycho is always in the south, and Ptolemæus near the middle. You will see, too, that the craters which are near the Moon's edge do not look round; they are oval – as with the 97 kilometre crater Plato, in the north part of the Moon, which has a very dark grey floor. Plato is not really oval; it is circular, but

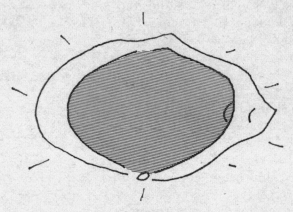

The lunar crater Plato

we are looking at it ('from the side', so to speak. Remember, the Moon is not flat. It is a ball, like the Earth. You can see why the craters seem oval by making a simple experiment. Take a football, draw circles on it, and then look at the football from the side; the circles which you have drawn near the top or bottom of the ball will look oval.

The reason why the craters and mountains keep in the same places is that the Moon spins round very slowly. Our 'day' is 24 hours long, so that the Earth takes 24 hours to spin round once; but the Moon takes just over 27 of our days. This is exactly the same time that the Moon needs to go once round the Earth, and the result is that it always keeps the same face turned towards us. There is a part of the Moon which we can never see from Earth.

The best way to explain this is to ask a friend to sit on a chair, and then walk round him, turning so as to keep your face turned towards him all the time. Your face stands for the part of the Moon which we can see, and the back of your neck stands for the Moon's 'other side'. When you have been round the chair once, you will have looked at every wall of the room in turn; but your friend will never have seen the back of your neck. In the same way, we on Earth can never see the 'back' of the Moon, because it is always turned away from us.

Until rockets were sent into space, we did not know quite what the other side of the Moon would be like. Now, of course, rockets carrying cameras and men have been round the Moon, and we have maps of the whole surface. The other side of the Moon is very like the side we can see. It has mountains, valleys and craters, though it does not have any of the large grey plains which we still call seas.

The Moon always keeps the same face turned towards the Earth, but it does not keep the same face turned towards the Sun. This means that the 'other side', too, has regular day and night. The main difference is that anyone standing on the Earth-turned side of the Moon will always see the Earth above the horizon, while anyone who goes to the far side of the Moon will never be able to see the Earth at all.

8

ROCKETS TO THE MOON

THE first stories about flying to the Moon were written a very long time ago, but it was not until our own time that men found out how to send up space-ships. No aircraft can fly more than a few tens of kilometres above the ground, because the air becomes too thin. Remember, even on the top of Mount Everest, which is less than 8 kilometres high, there is so little air that nobody can breathe it.

An aeroplane with a propeller works by gripping the air with its propeller, forcing the air underneath its wings, and using its wings to keep itself up. Without air, the propeller has nothing to grip. A jet-aircraft has to draw air into its motors to make it work. This is why no aircraft can fly above the top of the air. To go into space, we must use some kind of engine which does not need air round it. The only engine which can manage this is the rocket.

A firework rocket, of the kind fired in England on Guy Fawkes' Night (November the Fifth) is made up of a tube filled with gunpowder. When you light the gunpowder, it starts to burn, and it gives off hot gas. This gas rushes out of the rocket at one end, as shown in the picture, and as it does so it 'pushes' the rocket in the other direction, so that the rocket flies.

One way to show what happens is to take a balloon,

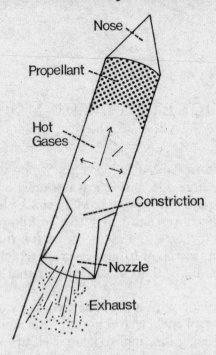

blow it up, and then let go the tube, as the boy in the next picture is doing. As the gas inside rushes out, the balloon shoots across the room. The balloon does not move in a straight line, because it has to push its way through the air; but in space there is no air.

Firework rockets are not very powerful, and cannot be used for space-travel. Instead, the rockets of today use motors of rather a different kind, and carry liquids instead of solid gunpowder, but the principles are just the same.

We know that the Earth's gravity tries to pull everything downwards, which is why we feel heavy. To break free from this pull, a rocket must go very fast indeed. It must, indeed, go at 11 kilometres a second – much faster

than any train or car. A train moving at 11 kilometres a second would be able to travel from London to Birmingham in only about a quarter of a minute.

If the rocket goes up at less than this speed, it will slow down, stop, and then fall back to the ground. If it starts off at 11 kilometres a second it will never come back, and it will escape from the Earth. It will be moving at what we call *escape velocity*.

The first space-rockets were fired less than thirty years ago, and the first real space-ship was not sent up until the year 1957. Since then there have been many more, most of them made by people working in America or Russia.

In 1961 a Russian, Yuri Gagarin, went up in a rocket and made a journey right round the Earth, so becoming the first _space-man_. During his flight he seemed to have no weight at all. If a man in a space-ship holds out a pencil and lets it go, the pencil will not fall, as it does on Earth; it simply stays where it is.

Many other space-men have been up in rockets since Gagarin's flight. The Americans even built a _space-station_, Skylab, and the last three men who went up to it stayed there for three months before coming down again. It used to be thought that a man would be harmed by staying up for so long, but this does not seem to be true. The three Americans were feeling quite strong and well when they landed after their long trip.

The first men to reach the Moon were also Americans; their names were Neil Armstrong and Edwin Aldrin, and they made their journey to the Moon in July 1969. Their space-ship was called Apollo 11. They started off from the rocket base in America; their ship was so big that it was as tall as St. Paul's Cathedral, but not all of it went to the Moon. The bottom part, with the most powerful motors, was used to send the top part away into space. Armstrong and Aldrin were in the top part, together with a third man, Michael Collins.

After two days the ship was close to the Moon. Then it was put into a path which took it round and round the Moon – just as the Moon itself goes round the Earth. Armstrong and Aldrin went into one part of the ship, leaving Collins behind, and used a separate rocket motor to take them down onto one of the Moon's grey plains. After landing, they put on space-suits and went outside.

Their suits had to be very carefully made; on the Moon, remember, there is no air.

They found a strange world. The sky is black even in the day-time, because there is no air to spread the sun-light around, and each 'day' lasts for as long as two of our weeks. On the Moon, a man weighs much less than he does at home, because the Moon has a much weaker pull of gravity. There are craters and pits everywhere, but there is no life.

Another strange thing about the Moon is that there can be no noise. Sound-waves are carried by air, and the airless Moon is always silent, though the space-men could talk to each other – and to people on Earth – by using the wireless sets built into their helmets.

After walking around, and picking up some rocks from the Moon to be brought home, the two men went back into their space-ship. They used their rocket motor to take off again, and joined the third member of the crew, Collins, who had been going round the Moon in the other part of the Apollo. Then they all came home, and landed in the sea, where they were picked up quite unhurt.

Since then, ten more men have been to the Moon and back. The later Apollo trips lasted for longer than the first, and the explorers were able to drive about the Moon in special cars which they took with them. Many rocks have been brought home, and have been carefully studied. We know much more about the Moon now than we did only a few years ago.

The last Apollo trip was made just before Christmas 1972. We do not know when the next men will go to the Moon, but it should be well before the year 2000, and plans are being made to set up a *Moon Base* where people can live and work. There is no reason why these plans should not succeed. I am sure that some of you who are reading this book will be able to go to the Moon, and see the mountains and craters for yourselves. In the sky, shining down at you, you will see the Earth – 400,000 kilometres away across space.

9

THE SUN

THE Sun is quite different from the Moon. As we have seen, the Moon goes round the Earth, and is a small world; it has no light or heat of its own. The Sun, on the other hand, is so big that it could swallow up more than a million Earths; it is very hot, and is made up of gas. It is nearly four hundred times as far away from us as the Moon, and the Earth moves round it, making one full journey in each year.

It is very dangerous to look straight at the Sun for more than a second or two. If you do so, you will hurt your eyes badly. To look at the Sun through a pair of binoculars, or a telescope, is even more dangerous, and means that you will blind yourself for ever. Remember this, because it is most important. I once knew an old man who had looked at the Sun through a telescope when he was eight years old – and for the rest of his life he was blind in one eye.

The danger comes not from the Sun's light, but from its heat. You can show this by using a magnifying-glass to focus the Sun's rays on to some paper or dry grass; if you do so, the paper or grass will catch alight – and this is one way in which Boy Scouts learn how to light a fire (though always be careful; if you start a fire in a field or a wood, during camp, you may do a great deal of damage). Just think what would happen if you let all this heat fall on to your eye!

Luckily, there is one way to use a telescope for studying the Sun. Point the telescope at the Sun, as the girl in the picture is doing, but without putting your eye anywhere near the tube. Then hold a piece of paper or white card behind the telescope, and you will see the Sun's image very well. This is safe enough if you are careful – but never try it for the first time unless there is someone with you to show you just how to do it.

The Sun's surface is bright yellow, and is made up of gas. On it you can sometimes see dark patches, which are known as *sunspots*. These spots are not really black; but they are less hot than the rest of the Sun, so that they look much darker than they really are. If you could see them shining by themselves, they would seem much brighter than the headlight of a car.

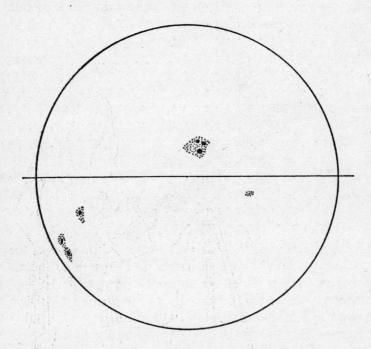

A sunspot is darkest near its middle; outside this there is a lighter part. Some spots are round, but others have no shape at all. Spots usually appear in groups. The picture here shows a large sunspot group. The size of the Earth is shown as a black circle, and you can see that a sunspot may be very much larger than the Earth.

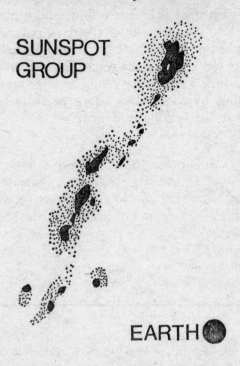

**SUNSPOT
GROUP**

EARTH

Like the Earth, the Sun spins round, but it does so much more slowly, and takes nearly a month to make one turn. If you look at sunspots from one day to another, you will find that they seem to move slowly across the Sun's face, because the Sun's rotation is carrying them along. After about two weeks, a spot will pass over the Sun's edge, and will not be seen again until about two weeks later, when it will come back into view round the opposite edge. When a spot lies near the edge of the Sun, it will look oval instead of round – for the same reason that a crater near the Moon's edge looks oval.

Because the Sun's surface is made of gas, no sunspot

lasts for very long. A big group may last for several months, but small spots often disappear after only a day or two. Storms on the Sun, often near spot groups, also cause the lovely glows in the Earth's upper air which we call *Polar Lights*. These lights are not very often seen from South England, but they can be very brilliant from Scotland or countries in the far north. Lights of the same kind are seen from places near the south pole of the Earth. Astronomers call them *auroræ*.

There are times when the Sun shows many spot-groups, and other times when there may be no spots at all. The Sun is at its most active every eleven years. The last really 'spotty' time was in 1969, so that we may expect many spots again about the year 1980.

The inside of the Sun is so hot that we cannot imagine what it must be like. The Sun is not burning in the same way as a fire, but is shining in quite a different way. In it there is a great deal of a light gas called *hydrogen*, and near the middle of the Sun very strange things are happening; the hydrogen is being changed into a different kind of gas, which is known as *helium*. Each time a little more helium is formed out of hydrogen, the Sun gives off energy and loses mass (which for the moment we can say is much the same thing as *weight*, though in fact there is an important difference). The energy given off keeps the Sun shining.

Astronomers have found out that the Sun is losing weight very quickly indeed. If you imagine a railway truck; suppose that it weighs ten tonnes. If you put four hundred thousand of these trucks together, they will weigh as much as the Sun is losing in every second of time.

Luckily, the Sun is so big that even this loss in weight does not matter very much. The Sun will go on shining for a very long time in the future, and it will look just the same when you have grown old as it does now. Indeed, it will not change noticeably for at least five thousand million years yet. Of course it will not go on shining for ever, but there is no need for anyone to become frightened. There is no chance that the Sun will suddenly go out!

10

WHEN THE SUN IS HIDDEN

THE Sun is much larger than the Moon, but it is also much further away from us, and in the sky the Sun and the Moon look just about the same size. You can see what is meant by going into the garden and taking with you a marble and a football. If you put the football far enough away, it will look no bigger than the marble which you hold at arm's-length.

Now let us go back to our diagram showing the Moon as it moves round the Earth. When the Moon is new, its dark side is turned towards us, and we cannot see it. But what will happen if the Moon gets in the way of the Sun? It will hide the Sun, and cause what we call a *solar eclipse*, or eclipse of the Sun.

EARTH   MOON   SUN

Remember that there is a great difference between an eclipse of the Moon and an eclipse of the Sun. Nothing can get in the way of the Moon, because there is nothing in the sky which is closer to us (unless we count the space-ships which have been sent up during the past twenty years). An eclipse of the Moon happens when the

Moon passes into the shadow thrown by the Earth. With a solar eclipse, the Sun is actually covered up.

The first thing to be noticed during an eclipse is that the Sun seems to have a 'bite' out of its edge; this is due to the dark body of the Moon, which we cannot see. Slowly the 'bite' becomes larger and larger, as shown in the drawings. If the Sun is completely hidden, the eclipse is total, and is a really wonderful sight. As soon as the last piece of the Sun's bright face is covered up by the Moon, we can see the Sun's atmosphere, which is usually invisible (though astronomers using special instruments have found out how to see it without waiting for an eclipse).

During a total eclipse you can see that the Sun is surrounded by what looks like mist. We call this the *corona*; it is made of gas, very much thinner than the air that you and I are breathing. At some eclipses you can also see red patches which look like flames, rising from the Sun's hidden surface. These are not really flames at all, but clouds of hot gas, known as *prominences*. As soon as the Moon moves away, and uncovers the first part of the Sun itself, the corona and the prominences disappear.

EARTH   MOON   SUN

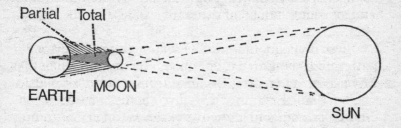

Not many of you will have seen a total eclipse of the Sun – because as seen from any one place on Earth, they do not happen often. The next diagram explains why. The shadow thrown by the Moon only just touches the Earth, so that to see a total eclipse you have to be in just the right place at just the right time. Also, a total eclipse does not last for long, and can never go on for much more than seven minutes, because the Moon keeps on moving.

The last total eclipse of the Sun to be seen from England took place in the year 1927. The next will not be until 11 August 1999, and even then you will have to go to Cornwall; from the rest of England the Sun will not be fully covered up, and the corona and the prominences will not be seen. Of course, there will be total eclipses before 1999 visible from other parts of the world, and astronomers are always ready to go on long journeys in order to study them. The last total eclipse that I saw was in June 1973; I was on board ship off the coast of North Africa.

We have found that eclipses of the Moon are not seen every month. For the same reason, we do not see eclipses of the Sun every time that the Moon is new. Usually, the new moon passes either above or below the Sun in the sky, so that there is no eclipse. There must be at least two solar eclipses each year, but not all of them are total, and, of course, not all of them are visible from the British Isles.

There is yet another kind of solar eclipse. The Moon's path round the Earth is not quite a circle, and when the Moon is at its greatest distance from us it looks a little smaller than the Sun. If the three bodies line up when the Moon is at its furthest away, the Moon cannot quite cover the Sun, and the outer bright edge of the Sun stays in view round the dark body of the Moon. This is known as an *annular eclipse*, because a ring of sunlight is left showing, and the Latin word for 'ring' was *annulus*. During an eclipse of this kind, the corona and the prominences cannot be seen.

There is no doubt that a total eclipse of the Sun is the most beautiful sight that anyone can see. The sky becomes so dark that stars come into view, and it is said that birds go to sleep, thinking that night has fallen. Men who lived long ago did not know the cause of eclipses, and were very frightened of them. The people of China believed that a dragon was trying to eat up the Sun – and as soon as an eclipse began, everyone would run out into the streets, shouting and screaming, and beating drums and gongs so as to scare the dragon away. There is an old story that two astronomers named Hi and Ho, who were in the service of an Emperor of China, once made a mistake and forget to tell the Emperor that an eclipse was due; the Emperor was so angry that he ordered their heads to be cut off! The story is probably not true, but it was not until much later in our history that astronomers came to know that solar eclipses are caused by the Moon passing in front of the Sun.

THE PLANETS

THE planets are the most important members of the Sun's family. As I have told you, the Earth comes third in order of distance. There are nine planets altogether, though not all of them are bright enough to be seen without a telescope.

The planets go round the Sun at different distances and in different times. The Earth goes round the Sun in $365\frac{1}{4}$ days, so that this is the length of our year. The planet closest to the Sun, Mercury, has a 'year' of only 88 days, while the furthest planet, Pluto, takes 248 of our years to make one full journey.

The planets look like stars when you see them in the night sky, but some of them are brighter than any of the real stars, and, of course, the planets move about from one star-group into another. As soon as you use a telescope, it is very easy to tell a planet from a star. A star looks just like a point of light, even if you are using a very powerful telescope, but a planet looks bigger, because it is so much closer to us.

Let me now give you the names of all the planets, beginning with Mercury and working outwards from the Sun. They are:

1. MERCURY, much smaller than the Earth, and never very bright; it is not easy to find, because it always stays close to the Sun in the sky.

2. VENUS, almost as big as the Earth. Venus is the brightest of all the planets, and is also the closest to us, though it is much further away than the Moon.

3. THE EARTH, with its one 'satellite', the Moon.

4. MARS, about half the diameter of the Earth, and very red. It can become very brilliant. It has two moons, though both are very small.

These four planets make up the inner group in the Sun's family or Solar System. Beyond the path of Mars there is a wide gap, in which move a great many small worlds which we call the minor planets or *asteroids*. Further away still, we come to:

5. JUPITER, much the biggest of all the planets; it is very bright, and is made up of gas, so that it is quite unlike the Earth. It has four large moons and nine small ones.

6. SATURN, also very large (though not so large as Jupiter). It, too, is made of gas. Saturn is the planet with the rings; it shines as a rather bright star, and is easy to find. It has ten satellites, though only one of them is as large as our Moon.

These were the only planets known before telescopes were first made. Since then we have found:

7. URANUS, another gas-giant; it is bigger than the Earth, but much smaller than Jupiter or Saturn. You can just see it with the naked eye (that is to say, without using binoculars or a telescope) if you know where to look for it. Binoculars show it easily. It has five moons, but none of them is very large.

8. NEPTUNE, still further away, and too faint to be seen without a telescope. It is very like Uranus, but it has only two moons, one large and the other small.

9. PLUTO, another small planet. It is so far away, and so faint, that we do not know much about it.

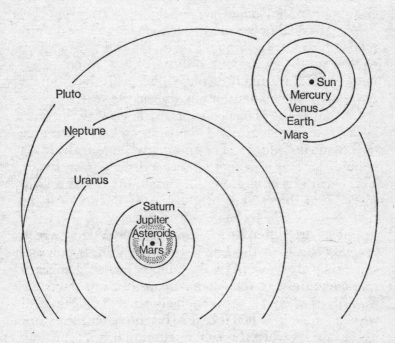

The diagram here shows the paths of the planets, and it is easy to see that the Solar System is divided into two parts, with the asteroids in between. Most of the planets move round the Sun in paths which are almost, though not quite, circular (remember that the Earth is a little closer to the Sun in December than in June). The only planet with a different kind of path is Pluto.

The planets have their paths in almost the same 'plane', so that if you could spread them out, as shown here, they would be more or less in a line. (Pluto, again, behaves rather differently.) This means that the planets seem to keep to a belt round the sky which we call the Zodiac; for instance, you can never see a planet in the famous star-group of the Great Bear, because the Great Bear is not in the Zodiac.

We always know where the planets will be at any moment, so it is easy to find them. All you have to do is to look up their positions and mark them in on a star-map. There are many books which will give you the positions of the planets for any time in the year.

Of course, the planets do not stay in view all the time, because they move round the Sun, and sometimes go over to the far side of it. For instance when Mars is almost behind the Sun it cannot be seen properly from Earth. Yet, when it is opposite to the Sun in the sky, it is well-placed and shines very brightly at night-time. All the planets beyond Mars behave in the same way.

Things are different for Mercury and Venus, which are closer in than the Earth. Since they shine only because they are being lit by the Sun, they show changes of shape like those of the Moon. Venus turns its dark side towards us when it is between the Earth and the Sun, and we cannot see it. When it is at its brightest, we see part of its sunlit side; when it is full, it is almost behind the Sun, so that it is invisible. Mercury moves in the same way. Through a telescope, Mercury and Venus may show up as tiny 'half-moons'.

All the planets are spinning round, so that they have their own days and nights, but they do not do so in 24 hours, as with the Earth. On Jupiter, the 'day' lasts for as long as several of our months. The only planet with a

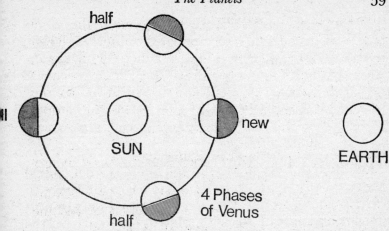

half

new

SUN

EARTH

half

4 Phases
of Venus

day much the same as ours is Mars, which spins round
once in 24½ hours.

Because the planets are at different distances from the
Sun, they move at different speeds. Mercury, the closest-
in of the planets, moves quickest; Neptune and Pluto, the
furthest out, move slowest.

Each planet has its own kind of year, day and climate.
We have found out a great deal about them, and we
have even sent rockets to some of them. One day, no
doubt, men will be able to go to them, but travelling to
the planets is much harder than travelling to the Moon,
because all the planets are so much further away from
us.

12

MERCURY, THE SMALLEST PLANET

THE closest of the planets to the Sun has been named Mercury. In the old stories, Mercury was the boy who carried messages for the gods, and was very quick-moving and difficult to catch. Mercury moves round the Sun more quickly than any of the other planets, and takes only 88 days to go once round.

It is not often that you can see Mercury easily without using a telescope, and if you happen to live in a town, with street lights around, you will have no hope of seeing it at all. It stays close to the Sun in the sky, and can be found only very low in the west after sunset or very low in the east before sunrise. When you find it, it will look like a rather bright star.

Mercury is much smaller than the Earth, and not very much bigger than the Moon. It has a weak pull of gravity, and it has no air, so that nothing can live there. It spins round very slowly, so that the 'day' on Mercury is much longer than ours; and it has no moon.

As I have told you, Mercury shows changes of shape like those of the Moon. Now and then it moves exactly between the Earth and the Sun, so that for a few hours it can be seen as a small black spot against the bright face of the Sun. This is called a *transit*. Transits do not happen very often, and the next one will not be seen until the year 1986.

Mercury is so small, and so far away, that no telescope will show much on its surface, and it was not until the first space-rocket was sent there that we found out what it is like. In 1974 an American rocket flew past Mercury, and sent back pictures showing that there are mountains, valleys and craters very much the same as those on the Moon.

If you could go to Mercury, the Sun would look much larger than it does from Earth, and during the daytime the rocks of Mercury would become so hot that if you put a tin kettle in the sunlight, the kettle would melt!

13

VENUS, THE BRIGHTEST PLANET

THE second planet from the Sun is called Venus, after the Goddess of Beauty in the old stories. Venus is indeed the most beautiful of the planets when seen without a telescope. Like Mercury, it seems to stay in the same part of the sky as the Sun, but it is much more brilliant than Mercury, because it is both larger and closer to us; it can stay above the horizon in the west for some hours after the Sun has set, and it may rise in the east well before the Sun does so. When at its brightest, it can even cast shadows.

Venus takes over seven months to go once round the Sun. If it passes directly between the Sun and the Earth, it is seen in transit as a black spot against the the Sun's

From Earth, Venus may be seen as a brilliant crescent moon.

face; but this is very unusual, and will not happen again until the year 2004.

Venus is almost as large as the Earth, but no telescope will show much on its surface; all you will usually see is a brilliant half, crescent or three-quarter 'moon'. This is because Venus has a thick, cloudy atmosphere, and we can see only the top part of it. It is always cloudy on Venus, and before rockets went there we did not know what the surface could be like. We did not even know the length of the 'day' on Venus. Some astronomers thought that the surface must be covered with water; other people believed that there was no water at all.

We know much more now, because the Americans have sent rockets past Venus, and the Russians have even landed space-probes there. These rockets have told us that the surface of Venus is so hot that nothing could live there. The atmosphere of the planet is not the same as our own air; it is made up of heavy gas which shuts in the Sun's heat.

The best way to explain this to think about what happens if you go into a greenhouse during a summer day. You will soon become very hot – because the glass of the greenhouse lets the rays of the Sun in, but will not let the heat out again. The gas round Venus does the same kind of thing, but Venus is much hotter than any greenhouse on Earth. On the surface, the temperature can go up to nearly a thousand degrees, so that Venus is even hotter than Mercury.

To make things even worse, the atmosphere of Venus presses down much more strongly than ours. If you went to Venus and stepped outside your space-ship, you would at once be poisoned, boiled and squashed! Venus does not seem to be the kind of world which anyone will ever be able to visit.

Though we can never see the true surface, we have been able to find out that there are big craters there. Mountains and valleys may also exist. There may even be active volcanoes, though we cannot yet be sure.

The first close-up pictures of Venus were sent back from an American space-rocket in 1974. These pictures showed the tops of the clouds, and from them astronomers were able to find out that these clouds move quite quickly, going once round Venus in only four days. Yet the planet itself spins very slowly. It takes 243 of our days to turn round once, and this is longer than the time which Venus takes to go round the Sun – so that the 'day' there is longer than the 'year'!

Nobody knows why this is so. To make things even more unusual, it has been found that Venus spins from east to west, not from west to east as the Earth and most of the other planets do. This means that if you could see the sky from the surface of Venus, the Sun would rise in the west, and set in the east four months later. In fact, however, the clouds would always hide the Sun. There could be no bright light, so that Venus must be a very gloomy kind of place.

The Russian space-ships which have landed there have come down through the planet's atmosphere by parachute, but the great heat has meant that messages from them stopped not long after they arrived, so that we do not yet know as much about Venus as we would like to do.

Unlike the Earth, Venus has no moon, so that it travels alone round the Sun.

14

MARS, THE RED PLANET

THE Earth is the third planet in order of distance from the Sun. Next comes Mars, which is perhaps the most interesting member of the Sun's family. It is very red, and so it was named after the old God of War; red is the colour of blood.

Mars is bigger than the Moon, but smaller than the

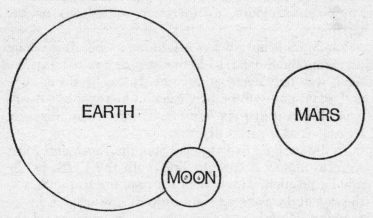

Earth. As can be seen from the picture, it comes about half-way in size between the Moon and the Earth. It is not so 'heavy' as the Earth; if you could put the Earth in one pan of a pair of scales, you would need ten planets such as Mars to balance it. This means that the pull of gravity on Mars is less than it is on our own world, and anyone going there will feel very light indeed. If you weigh 38 kilograms on the Earth, you will weigh only 12.5 kilograms on Mars.

Another result of this weak pull is that Mars has only a thin 'air'; and this 'air' is not made up of the same gases as ours. Long ago, Mars may have had more atmosphere than it has today, but much of this atmosphere has leaked away into space. The Moon and Mercury, which are smaller than Mars and pull even less strongly, have lost all of the air they may once have had.

Mars is easy to find in the sky when it is at its brightest. It is then more brilliant than any other planet except Venus, and its strong red colour means that you cannot mistake it. The surface of Mars really is red, and there are no thick clouds, as there are on Venus or the Earth.

Yet Mars is not always bright, and when it is a long way from the Earth it looks like an ordinary red star. We see it well only every other year. It was bright in 1971 and 1973, and will be bright again in 1975, but it was never brilliant in 1972 or 1974. To show why this is so, let us look at the next diagram.

In the summer of 1973, the Sun, the Earth and Mars were in almost a straight line, with the Earth in the middle position. Mars was then opposite to the Sun in the sky, and was very bright indeed. A year later, in the summer of 1974, the Earth had been once round the Sun, and had come back to the same position in its path – but Mars had not finished its journey. It has a 'year' of 687 Earth-days, and in the summer of 1974 it was still almost on the far side of the Sun. Not until near the end of 1975 will the three bodies be lined up again.

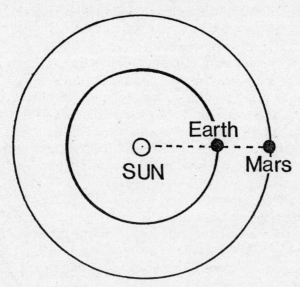

In 1973, the Sun, the Earth and Mars were almost in a straight line.

Because Mars is not a big planet, we need powerful telescopes to see it really well, but even if you have only a small telescope you will be able to make out markings on it when it is bright. (Binoculars will not be strong enough, though they will show that Mars is different from a star.) The first things you will notice, if you use a good telescope, will be the dark patches on the surface, and the white *caps* over the poles.

If you could look at the Earth from space, you would be able to see the white ice and snow at the north and south poles (if, of course, there were no thick clouds about). The same happens with Mars. During winter on Mars, the white patches are large and bright. When spring comes, the patches start to shrink, and in the middle of the summer on Mars they almost disappear.

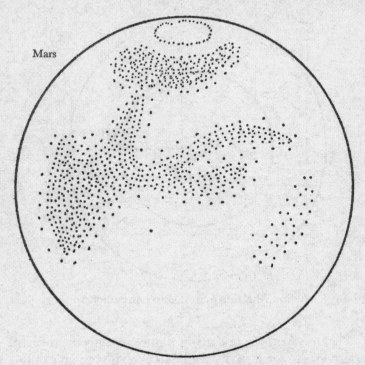

Mars

Because the white patches at the poles of Mars behave in this way, it was once thought that they too must be made up of ice and snow, but this does not seem to be true. There may be some ordinary ice, but most astronomers now think that the caps are made mostly of what is called *solid carbon dioxide* – much the same as the dry ice you see in an ice-cream seller's barrow. This seems quite likely, because most of the thin atmosphere of Mars is made up of carbon dioxide gas.

The dark patches are always to be seen, except when there are great dust-storms in the atmosphere of Mars. They do not change much in shape, and they have been carefully mapped. They cannot be seas, because water cannot exist on the surface of the planet; the air is too thin. It was once thought that the dark patches were old sea-bottoms filled with plants, but the space-rockets sent

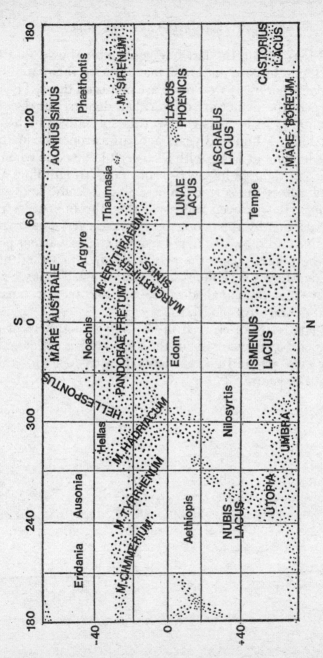

Map of Mars

to Mars during the last few years have shown that the dark patches are not low-lying. Some of them are high, and it is not likely that there are plants on them. The red parts of the planet are often called deserts, but they are not hot. Mars is a very cold world, especially at night.

Almost a hundred years ago, an astronomer in Italy was looking at Mars with a powerful telescope when he saw – or thought he saw! – some long, straight lines running across the surface. These lines became known as *canals*. It was even suggested that the lines were real canals, dug by the people on Mars to carry water from the ice and snow at the poles down to the warmer parts of the planet where the people lived. This would have made Mars a very interesting place indeed, but we now know that the canals do not exist, and we can be sure that nobody lives on Mars.

Clouds are often seen in the thin atmosphere of the planet, but they are not of the same kind as the clouds in our own air, and no rain has fallen on Mars for thousands of years.

15

THE VOLCANOES OF MARS

BOTH the Americans and the Russians have sent space-ships to Mars. We have found out most from Mariner 9, which was sent up from America in the year 1971. When the rocket was close to Mars, its motor was used to put it into a path round the planet. Of course there were no men on board, but there were cameras, and the pictures taken by these cameras were sent back to Earth by tele-vision.

Astronomers were surprised at what they saw. The first space-ships had already told us that Mars has craters on its surface, not very different from those of the Moon; but the new pictures showed that there were also high volcanoes, together with deep valleys. The highest of these volcanoes has its top about 24 kilometres above the ground below. This is much taller than our Everest, which is less than 8 kilometres high.

Away from the volcanoes, the picture showed valleys which looked as though they had been made by running water, and there were also markings which looked very like old river-beds. This was not what had been ex-pected. As we know, there can be no water on Mars now, and so there can be no rivers – but the river-beds did not look very old, because they were not worn away or filled up by the dust which is blown about in the atmosphere of Mars.

Some astronomers think that Mars has *dry periods* and *wet periods*. During a wet period, which may last for some thousands of years, the atmosphere becomes thicker for a while, and rain falls. Then the atmosphere leaks away into space, because the weak pull of gravity on Mars cannot hold it down; the water disappears, and Mars becomes dry again, as it is today. If this idea is right, Mars may have another wet period in the future. Of course, this whole picture may be wrong, and in any case we do not know just why such wet periods should happen.

Mars is a cold world. Even in the middle of a summer day at the equator, the heat can never be greater than that in London in spring or autumn, and the nights are very cold, because the thin air cannot shut in much of the Sun's warmth. If you could go to Mars, you would have to wear a space-suit all the time, and you would have to take all your air and water with you.

But though we could not breathe on Mars, we cannot yet be sure that there is no life there. It is just possible that there may be plants of a kind, though most astronomers do not think it very likely. The only way to find out is to land a rocket gently on the surface of the planet, so that it can send back messages and tell us what it finds. The Americans have made plans to do this, and they hope to land a rocket there in 1976. Then, at last, we should be able to answer the question which we have been asking for so long: Is there any life on Mars?

Even if no life is found, we may still hope to send men to Mars within the next fifty years or so. After all, Mars is much less unfriendly than Venus. There is no dense, poisonous atmosphere, and the climate is much less hot. If all goes well, bases will be set up there, in which men and women will spend all their lives. This will not happen yet, but it should certainly happen in the future.

We have only one moon. Mars has two; they are called Phobos and Deimos. Both are very small, and both are close to Mars. Phobos, the brighter of the two, is shown on some of the pictures sent back from the American space-ship Mariner 9; it is only 26 kilometres long and 19 kilometres wide, so that it can give very little light during a night on Mars. Its surface is covered with small craters, and it looks just like a lump of rock. It goes round Mars in only $7\frac{1}{2}$ hours. If you looked at it from the surface of Mars, Phobos would rise in the west, cross the sky the wrong way, and set in the east a few hours later; it would do this three times a day. Deimos, the other moon, is even smaller than Phobos, and is of the same type. From Mars it would look rather like a large, pale star. From Earth, you need a powerful telescope to see either Phobos or Deimos.

16

THE LITTLE PLANETS

MARS is the last of the small planets fairly close to the Sun. Jupiter, the first of the giant worlds, is much further away. Between the paths of Mars and Jupiter there is a wide gap, and astronomers of long ago thought that there really should be a planet there.

At last a group of astronomers set to work to look for the missing planet. They knew that it must be too faint to be seen without a telescope, or it would have been found already; they did not know where it was, or even if it really existed. But in 1801, even before they had begun to hunt, an astronomer in the island of Sicily was mapping the stars when he came across something which moved slowly from night to night. He knew that it could not be a star, and it turned out to be a new planet, moving in a path beyond that of Mars. It was named Ceres, after the guardian goddess of Sicily in the old stories.

Ceres is very small; we know now that it is about 1300 kilometres across. In a telescope it looks just like a star, and it is much too small to have any air round it. The 'planet-hunters' wondered whether it were the only world in that part of the Solar System, and so they kept on searching. They soon found three more planets, all smaller than Ceres; they were named Pallas, Juno and Vesta. A few years later they gave up the hunt, but in

1845 a fifth small planet was found, and others followed. By now we know more than three thousand of these little asteroids, as they are called, and no doubt more will be discovered in the future.

Not many of the asteroids are as much as a hundred miles across, and most of them are very small indeed. The brightest asteroid is Vesta, even though it is not as big as Ceres; you can just see it without using a telescope or binoculars when it is at its best.

All the larger asteroids keep to the part of the Solar System in between the paths of Mars and Jupiter, as shown here, but there are some smaller asteroids which move differently. A few of them are just as far from the Sun as Jupiter itself. Others can swing in towards the Earth, and come quite near us, though we do not know of any asteroid which has come as close as the Moon.

Eros is one of these unusual asteroids. It is shaped rather like a sausage, and is less than 32 kilometres long. It last passed by us early in 1975, though of course it never became bright. In the year 1937 an even smaller asteroid, Hermes, came within 80 thousand kilometres of us – and when the news became known, some people were afraid that it might hit the Earth. In fact, there is almost no danger that an asteroid will hit us. This is lucky, because if an asteroid landed on a town or city it would kill many people.

How were the asteroids born? We do not really know. They may be the pieces of an old planet which broke up a long time ago, but it is more likely that the asteroids were simply 'left over' when the Earth and the other large planets were formed out of the cloud of dust and gas which once surrounded the Sun.

If you could land on an asteroid, you would seem to have very little weight, because even Ceres has a weak pull of gravity. If you jumped upwards, you would reach a great height before you started to come down again, and you would fall very slowly indeed. If you jumped off one of the smallest asteroids, you would never come down at all – and you would sail away into space. We do not yet know whether men will ever be able to visit asteroids, but at least space-rockets should be able to send back close-up pictures of them before many years have passed by.

17

JUPITER, THE GIANT PLANET

WELL beyond the main group of asteroids we come to Jupiter, the giant of the Sun's family. It is so big that it could swallow up more than a thousand bodies the size of the Earth, and it has a very strong pull of gravity. Because it is so large, it shines very brightly in our sky. It is usually more brilliant than any of the other planets apart from Venus, and it can be well seen for several months in every year.

Jupiter is quite different from the Earth. Instead of having a solid surface made up of rocks, its outer parts are made of gas. Jupiter may have no true solid surface at all, though near its centre the gas must be very dense. We also think that Jupiter is hot inside, though the outer gas is very cold because the planet is so far from the Sun.

If you look at Jupiter through even a small telescope, you will see that it is not round but flattened. We know why this is so. Though it has a 'year' almost twelve times as long as ours, Jupiter is spinning round very quickly; a 'day' there lasts for less than ten hours. This quick spin makes the equator bulge out. We have also found that the 'day' is not the same length all over the planet; it is shortest near the equator, and about five minutes longer near Jupiter's poles.

Since its surface is made of gas, Jupiter has no lands or

seas. It is crossed by lines which we call *cloud belts*, showing up clearly beside the brighter parts of the planet to either side. The belts do not always look the same, but generally at least two can be seen with a small telescope.

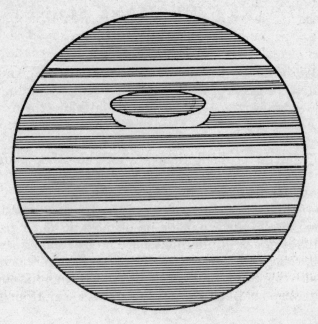

Spots are also seen on Jupiter. Most of them last for only a few weeks or months before disappearing, but there is one which has been on view for a very long time. This is the *Great Red Spot*; it was first observed over 300 years ago. Its colour really is red, and at its largest the Spot has a surface which covers more square miles than the surface of the Earth. Sometimes the Red Spot disappears for a year or two, but it always comes back.

It used to be thought that the Red Spot might be a kind of island floating in gas, but now seems more likely be the top of a very tall stream of gas coming from deep inside Jupiter. Nobody knows why it looks so red.

Two space-ships have been sent to Jupiter. The first, Pioneer 10, passed by the planet in December 1973 at a distance of only about 129,000 kilometres – and this is less than the diameter of Jupiter itself. Pioneer was not meant to land on Jupiter; a landing would be impossible, because one cannot bring a rocket down onto a layer of gas! After passing by the planet, Pioneer 10 went on into space, and is now on its way out of the Solar System altogether.

Much was found out from the signals sent back by Pioneer. We learned a great deal about Jupiter's magnetic field, and some of the pictures showed the cloud belts and the Red Spot very well indeed.

Pioneer 11 followed Pioneer 10 a year later. After passing by Jupiter, at the end of 1974, it was sent on to the next planet, Saturn; but it has a long way to go, and it will not reach Saturn before the year 1979. Both the Pioneers will go on into space for ever, and will never come back to the Sun. As soon as their radio signals become too weak to be heard, we will lose all track of them, and we will never know what happens to them.

18

THE MOONS OF JUPITER

JUPITER has more moons or satellites than any other planet. There are thirteen of them altogether, though only four are big.

The four bright moons were discovered very soon after telescopes were first made – which was a long time ago, when James I was King of England. One of the first astronomers to use a telescope was an Italian named Galileo. His telescope was not nearly so good as a pair of

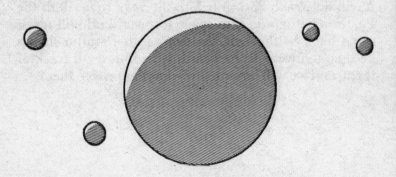

binoculars in use today, but it showed him four starlike points close to Jupiter, and he soon found that they followed Jupiter along, so that they could not be real stars. The four moons were given names: Io, Europa, Ganymede and Callisto. The first two are about the same size as our Moon, but Ganymede and Callisto are larger, and are almost as big as the planet Mercury.

If you have a telescope, you can watch the four moons as they change in position from night to night. You will not always see all four. If one of them is in front of Jupiter, it will be hard to see against the bright face of the planet; if it is behind Jupiter it will, of course, be out of view; and the moons may also move into Jupiter's shadow, so that the sunlight is cut off from them and they are eclipsed – just as our Moon is sometimes eclipsed by the shadow of the Earth.

Pioneer 10 sent back pictures of two of the moons (Io and Ganymede), but the pictures were not very clear, and we must hope that future space-ships will do better. Even Ganymede, the largest of the four, has too weak a pull of gravity to hold on to any air which would be thick enough for us to breathe, and, of course, Jupiter's great distance from the Sun means that all its moons are very cold. It is thought that Callisto is partly covered with a sheet of ice.

The other nine moons are so small that they cannot be seen except with powerful telescopes. One of them is very close to Jupiter, but the rest are further out than Callisto. The four small satellites which are furthest from Jupiter move round the planet 'the wrong way', rather like a car going the wrong way in a roundabout; but there is no danger that any of the moons will hit each other.

Men will never be able to land on Jupiter, but it is quite possible that in the future it will be possible to go to some of the satellites, even though we will need rockets much better than those we can build today.

Good binoculars will often show Io, Europa, Ganymede and Callisto; and if you have a telescope, you will find Jupiter one of the most interesting things in the sky. It is, after all, the largest and most important planet in the Sun's family.

19

SATURN AND ITS RINGS

FAR outside the path of Jupiter we come to Saturn. It, too, is a giant world. It is not so big as Jupiter, but it is much larger than the Earth. It is also the most beautiful of the planets, because of its rings.

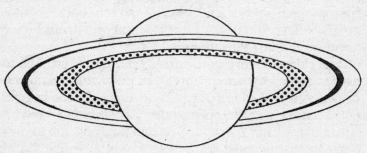

Saturn is brighter than most of the stars, and, like Jupiter, it can be well seen for several months in every year; but it is not brilliant enough to stand out in the same way that Jupiter and Venus do. It is rather yellow, and does not twinkle so much as a star. Once you have found it, you will always be able to recognize it again.

Like Jupiter, Saturn has a surface which is made up of gas, but this gas is not so dense as that of Jupiter. Saturn 'weighs' much less than might be thought. It is less dense than water – so that if you could put Saturn into a huge ocean, it would float! Cloud belts can be seen on it, and sometimes there are spots, but there is nothing like the Great Red Spot on Jupiter.

The 'year' on Saturn is 29 times as long as ours. The 'day' is only a little over ten hours long, so that Saturn too spins round very quickly.

Binoculars will show that there is something unusual about the shape of Saturn, and if you have a telescope you will be able to see the wonderful rings. These rings are not solid. They are made up of small pieces of rock or ice, all moving round Saturn, and so small and so close together that when we look at them from Earth the rings seem solid. In fact there are three rings; two of them are bright, and there is a gap between them, while the inner ring is much fainter and less easy to see. Some astronomers believe that one or two more rings exist, but I have never been able to see them myself.

The rings are very thin, and when they are edge-on to us we cannot see them properly. In the picture, Saturn is drawn as it looked in 1974 (A) and as it will look in 1980 (B). To show what happens, takes a postcard and hold it out at arm's-length, first face-on and then edge-on to your eyes. When the card is edge-on, it will look like a thin line. Saturn's rings behave in the same way, and when edge-on to us they are difficult to see at all, even with powerful telescopes.

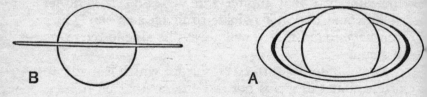

We do not really know how Saturn's rings were formed, but two suggestions have been made. It may be that the rings are all that is left of an old moon of Saturn which went too close to the planet, and was broken up by the strong pull of gravity. Other astronomers think that the rings were never part of a larger body.

In any case, Saturn still has ten moons left, and one of them, Titan, is bright enough to be seen in a small telescope. It is larger than any of the satellites of Jupiter, and is important because it is the only moon in the Solar System known to have atmosphere. Indeed, the atmosphere of Titan is much thicker than the atmosphere of Mars, though it is not made up of gas which we could breathe. Nobody could live on Titan, and of course it is a very cold world, because it is so far away from the Sun.

It is not easy to send a space-ship out as far as Saturn, but Pioneer 11, which passed by Jupiter at the end of 1974, is on its way there. If its cameras are still working by the time that it arrives near Saturn, we will have our first close-up pictures of the rings. It would be dangerous for a space-ship to go too near the rings, because of the risk of being hit by some of the pieces of rock and ice.

There is no doubt that Saturn is the most beautiful planet in the Sun's family, and perhaps the most beautiful thing in the whole sky. There is nothing else known to us which is at all like the Ringed Planet.

20

URANUS

ALMOST two hundred years ago, an astronomer named William Herschel was busy mapping the stars with a reflecting telescope that he had made himself. Astronomy was his greatest interest, but he earned his living by teaching music and playing the organ, so that he had to work hard by day and look at the stars by night.

Suddenly he found something which did not look at all like a star. When he saw it again the next night, he found that it had moved. He did not know what it was; but when its path was worked out, it was found to be a new planet, much further away from the Sun than Saturn. It was named Uranus, after another of the gods in the old stories.

If you have keen eyes, you will just be able to see Uranus without using binoculars or a telescope, but it will look only like a faint star. Yet Uranus is a giant planet. It is much bigger than the Earth, though smaller than Jupiter or Saturn. It is green in colour, and it has five satellites, though all of them are smaller than our Moon.

Uranus takes 84 years to go round the Sun. It has a short 'day' of less than eleven hours long, but it spins in an unusual way. It is tipped right over, as shown in the diagram, and sometimes one of its poles is pointed straight towards us. No other planet behaves like this, and we do not know why Uranus is tilted on to its side.

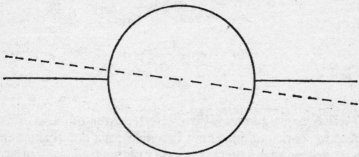

The axis of Uranus is shown by the dotted line. The direction of the planet's movement round the Sun is shown by the solid line.

No telescope will show much on Uranus, but we know that its surface, like those of Jupiter and Saturn, is made up of gas, so that it will never be possible to send a rocket there. In the future we may be able to land on some of the five moons, but this will not be done yet. Uranus is so far away that a rocket of the kind we can build at present would take years to reach it.

21

NEPTUNE

WHEN a new planet is discovered, astronomers do their best to work out just how it will move. For this, they have to find what effects the other planets will have on it. Each planet pulls upon each other planet; for example, the Earth does not travel round the Sun in quite the path that it would follow if Venus and the rest of the planets did not exist.

Uranus was found in the year 1781, and for a time all seemed to be well. Then Uranus began to move away from the path which it had been expected to follow. Astronomers did not know what was the matter; they worked out their sums again, but still Uranus would not move as it should have done. It was suggested that there might be a planet still further away from the Sun, which was pulling Uranus out of position – but where could this planet be?

Two astronomers, one in England and one in France, started to work out the position of the unknown planet. It was rather like a detective story; they could see the 'victim', Uranus, and they had to track down the planet which was causing all the trouble.

The Englishman, John Adams, finished first. He did not have a telescope of his own, but he believed that he knew just where the new planet must be, and he sent his work to the Astronomer Royal, whose name was Airy.

Unfortunately Airy was not very interested, and for a time nothing was done.

The Frenchman, Le Verrier, did not know about what Adams had been doing. He finished his work a little later, and sent it to the observatory at Berlin, in Germany. Airy heard the news, and asked one of his astronomers to begin looking in the place which Adams had given. He was too late. At Berlin the new planet was quickly found, looking like a faint star, but showing movement from one night to the next. It was named Neptune, after the god of the sea in the old legends.

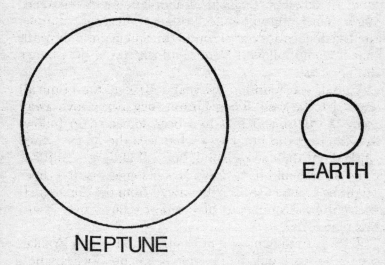

NEPTUNE

EARTH

Neptune is a little larger than Uranus, and much bigger than the Earth. It is very much like Uranus, though it is not tipped on to its side in the same way. It is much further from the Sun, so that it is very cold indeed. Neptune looks blue when seen through a powerful telescope, but in binoculars or a small telescope it seems just like a star.

Neptune has two moons. One of them is very small, but the other, Triton, is larger than our Moon, and is brighter than any of the five satellites of Uranus.

No space-ship to Neptune has been planned yet, but one will certainly be sent there in the future. The journey will be a long one. Neptune itself takes over 164 years to make one trip round the Sun!

22

PLUTO, THE COLDEST PLANET

THE last of the nine planets is named Pluto. It is so faint that it cannot be seen without a powerful telescope, and we do not know very much about it.

Pluto was discovered in the same way as Neptune; its position was worked out before the planet was seen. The discovery was made by an American named Clyde Tombaugh, in 1930. Tombaugh was then a young man; he is still working hard as an astronomer, and he visited England a little while ago.

Pluto is a very unusual planet. It is not a giant, and it is thought to be smaller than the Earth. It moves round the Sun in a path which can bring it closer-in than Neptune, as you can see from the next diagram, but there is no danger that Pluto will hit Neptune, because its path is tilted. The two planets do not pass close to each other.

Pluto takes 248 years to go round the Sun, so that if you lived there you would have to wait 248 Earth-years for your first birthday. Of course, Pluto is so cold that there can be no life on it. Even air of the kind we breathe would turn into a liquid on Pluto.

In the old stories, Pluto was the God of the Underworld, and the planet named after him is so far away that it must be very gloomy. Even the Sun would look only like a brilliant star, though it would still give much more light than the full moon does on Earth. There may

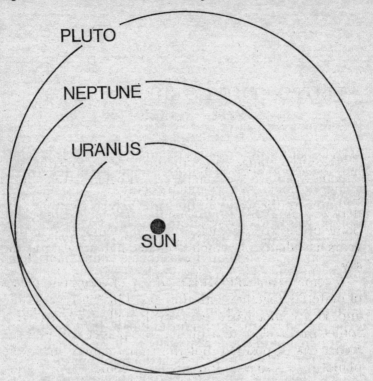

be mountains, valleys and even craters on Pluto, but as yet we do not know, and we will not find out until the first space-ship goes there and sends back pictures. Even a radio wave would take more than five hours to travel from Pluto to the Earth.

It is quite possible that there is another planet in the Solar System, moving further out than Pluto. Some astronomers have even been trying to find out where it may be; but it will be very faint and hard to find even if it is really there. So far as we know at present, Neptune and Pluto are the two furthest-away planets of the Sun's family.

23

THE COMETS

UNUSUAL things can sometimes be seen in the sky. Among them are the comets, which belong to the Sun's family, but are quite different from the planets. A comet may become really bright, and it may have a long tail. Some of the great comets which have appeared in past years have had tails which stretched half-way across the sky.

A comet is not solid. It is made up of very small pieces of material, together with thin gas. This gas is very thin, and so a comet has a very weak pull of gravity. If a comet passes close to a planet, the planet will pull the comet out of position, but the comet cannot move the planet; this is so even for very large comets. One comet, seen over a hundred years ago, was bigger than the Sun, but it did not 'weigh' very much compared with even a small planet. Its tail was 322 million kilometres long – more than twice the distance between the Earth and the Sun.

Though comets are members of the Solar System, most of them move round the Sun in paths which are not in the least like circles. The shape of a comet's path is an *ellipse* – or, if you like, a 'stretched-out circle'. You can make an ellipse by taking an elastic band and pulling it out. (In fact the Earth also moves in an ellipse, not a circle; but as we have seen, our distance from the Sun does not change very much.)

The comet whose path is shown in the next drawing is called Halley's Comet, because its movements were first worked out by a great astronomer named Edmond Halley. It takes 76 years to go once round the Sun, so that for a few months every 76 years we see it shining brightly; it then has a long tail. Records of it go back before the time of Christ; it was seen again in 1066, when William the Conqueror was making ready to attack England. It last returned in 1910, and we know that it will be back once more in 1986, but at the moment we cannot see it, because it is still too far away. A comet shines because it is lit up by the Sun, and when it is a long way from us it is too faint to be observed.

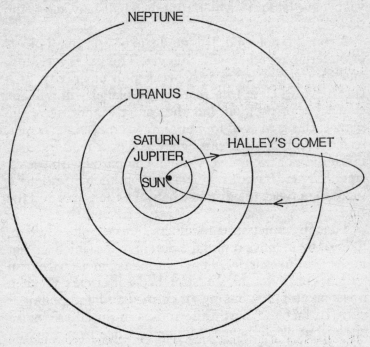

If you see something travelling quickly across the sky, it cannot be a comet. A comet lies well outside the Earth's atmosphere, and unless you watch it for many hours you will not be able to notice that it is moving at all against the background of stars. A moving object must be closer to us than any comet.

There are many comets which take only a few years to go round the Sun, and we always know when to expect them, but all of them are faint. Apart from Halley's, all bright comets take so long to make one journey that we never know when they will appear. There have been no really brilliant comets for some years now, though there have been several which have become visible with the naked eye. We had hoped to see a bright comet about Christmas-time in 1973; it had been found by an astronomer named Kohoutek, and it caused a great deal of interest, but unfortunately it turned out to be much fainter than had been expected. By now it has moved away from the Sun, and we can no longer see it at all. It will not come back for about 75,000 years!

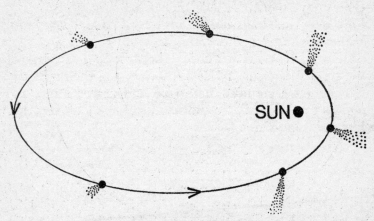

The direction of a comet's tail. The tail always points more or less away from the Sun.

A large comet is made up of a head and tail. The tail is made of gas which is even thinner than that in the head, together with tiny pieces of what we can call *dust* even though it is not like the dust you will find in a room which has not been cleaned. A comet's tail always points more or less away from the Sun, so that when a comet is moving outward it travels tail-first. However, not all comets have tails, and many of them look like nothing more than small patches of 'fog' in the sky.

People used to be afraid of comets, and thought that they were unlucky. It was also believed that a comet would break up the Earth if it hit us. Of course, this is not so. A comet is not at all unlucky, and it could not break up the Earth, though it is true that a direct hit could cause a great deal of damage. Some astronomers think that a small comet really did hit the Earth in the year 1908. It landed in Siberia, and blew trees flat for many kilometres round the point where it came down, but fortunately nobody was killed.

We never know when a bright comet will appear; there may be one this year, next year – or, perhaps, not for a long time to come. We may even have to wait until Halley's Comet comes back in 1986. It is a pity that brilliant comets are so unusual, because they are some of the most interesting objects to be seen in the night sky. One comet, seen more than two hundred years ago, had no less than six tails, so that it must have looked rather like a shining fan.

24

SHOOTING-STARS

IF you look up into a dark, clear sky for a few minutes any time during the first part of August, you may see some bright streaks of light which move quickly across the sky and then disappear. These are meteors, or shooting-stars. August is the best time of the year for seeing them, though meteors may appear at other times also.

A meteor is nothing like a star. As we know, a star is a sun, and our Sun is only a star. A meteor is a tiny object, usually smaller than a pin's head, moving round the Sun in the same way as a planet. So long as it stays well away from us, we cannot see it; but if it comes close to the Earth it flashes into the top part of our air. It has to push the air out of its way, and this causes 'friction', which in turn causes heat. You can make an experiment to show what friction means. Rub your hands together very quickly, and you will soon find that they are becoming warm, because of the friction of one hand against the other.

When a meteor comes into the air, it is travelling so quickly that it becomes hot and bursts into flame. It burns away, and it is this which causes the streak of light in the sky. In a second or two the meteor has burned away. The name 'shooting-star' is not really a good one for it!

Most meteors travel round the Sun in swarms, and

each time the Earth passes through a swarm of meteors we see a shower of shooting-stars. If you watch the August meteors, you will be able to tell that they seem to come from one special part of the sky. This the area of the constellation which we call Perseus, and so the August meteors are called the Perseids. (I will say more about the constellations in *Let's Look at the Sky! The Stars.*)

The best way to show why this happens is to picture the view you have from a bridge overlooking a motor-

way. If you look down the motorway, you will see that all its roads seem to meet at a point near the horizon. Cars coming down the motorway towards you will seem to be coming from this point, even though the roads are really parallel – that is to say, keeping the same distance from each other. (Otherwise, the cars would collide!) The meteors of a swarm are moving through space in parallel paths, and so they too seem to come from one special point, which we call the *radiant*.

The August Perseids give us the best shower in each year, but you may well see some meteors on any clear night. If you see a meteor which outshines any star or planet, it is not easy to remember that it is so small. What we are really seeing is not the meteor itself, but the hot air which it causes as it burns away. It may leave a trail for several seconds, but then this, too, disappears.

Now and then a really splendid shower is seen. The best one of recent years took place in November 1966, when for a few hours meteors seemed to fall down as thickly as snowflakes. Unfortunately this shower was not seen in England, because it took place in our daytime, but it was well seen from parts of America.

I have told you that there is a great difference between a meteor and a comet. A comet lies well beyond the Earth's atmosphere, so that you cannot see it shifting against the stars unless you watch it for many hours. A meteor is seen only when it is inside the Earth's air, and is burning away. Yet there is a connection between meteors and comets – and meteor swarms move along the same paths as comets. It has even been said that meteors are due to the breaking-up of old comets.

This was once seen to happen. More than a hundred years ago astronomers knew of a comet which used to take almost seven years to go round the Sun; it was

called Biela's Comet, because it had been discovered by
an Austrian named Biela. Then the comet broke in half,
so that instead of one comet there were two, travelling
round the Sun together. After this, both the comets dis-
appeared – but from the place where they should have
been there came a shower of shooting-stars. Each November we still see a few meteors which come from the
dead comet.

Nobody can tell just when or where a shooting-star
will be seen, and it lasts for only a very short time before
it burns away. But if you look up into a dark, clear sky
you may see a meteor at any time, and during the first
weeks of August there are plenty of them. It is almost as
though you can watch a display of 'sky fireworks'.

25

STONES FROM THE SKY

ON Christmas Eve, 1965, a bright light was seen over many places in England. Something shot across the sky, and pieces of stone landed in and near Barwell, a small village in Leicestershire. This was a meteorite. It came from outer space, and had been moving around in the Solar System for millions of years before it hit the Earth.

Many meteorites have been found, and a few have even been seen to fall in the same way as that at Barwell. Some of them are made up of stone, while others are heavier, and are made chiefly of iron. Before men learned how to use rockets, these meteorites were the only things from space which we could study on Earth – though now, of course, we can collect and bring back rocks from the Moon.

A meteorite comes into the Earth's air in the same way as a shooting-star meteor, but it is much bigger, and so it can land without being burned away. It may break up during its fall, but really large meteorites can land as huge lumps. One, found in Africa, weighs over 60 tonnes.

It is not true to say that a meteorite is simply a very large meteor. There is a great difference, and meteorites are much more like the asteroids which move round the Sun between the paths of Mars and Jupiter. They do not belong to showers, and we do not think that they come from broken-up comets. Like the asteroids, they may be made up of material 'left over' when the Earth and the other main planets were formed.

If you go to a museum, you can see meteorites of all kinds. They have been carefully collected and studied, and we have learned a great deal from them. Remember, though, that it is not easy to tell a meteorite from an ordinary piece of material just by looking at it; and so if you find a piece of iron or stone lying around do not think at once that it must have come from the sky.

A very large meteorite may make a crater when it lands. The best-known of these craters is in Arizona, in the United States; it is almost a mile wide, and is quite deep. If you go there, you can climb down inside it – but it takes a long time to climb back out of the crater. We do not know when it was formed, but it must have existed well before any men lived in that part of America. There are other known meteorite craters, some of which are to be found in Australia.

If a large meteorite hit a town or a city, many people would be killed, but luckily this is not likely to happen. Big meteorites are very rare. One hit Siberia in 1947, and I have already told you about the 1908 explosion, also in Siberia, which may have been due either to a meteorite or to the head of a small comet. There is no known case of anyone having been killed by a meteorite, though some years ago a woman in America had a narrow escape – she was lying in bed when a meteorite came in through the roof of her room, crashed through the floor and landed in the cellar below!

If you go and look at a meteorite, remember that you are seeing something which is very old indeed, and which has travelled a long way. Its journey between the planets has lasted for millions of years. It is not surprising that everyone is interested in these strange stones which come from the sky.

The Solar System, then, is a wonderful place. We have the Sun itself – a great ball of hot gas, shining at a furious rate. We have the planets, of which the Earth is one; we have the moons, the asteroids, the comets, the shooting-stars, and the meteorites which end their careers by landing on the surface or our world. There is much to see, as you will soon find if you go outdoors and look. Above all, do not forget that the Solar System is of special importance to us. It is our home in the universe.

SOME USEFUL TERMS

ASTEROID. A very small planet. Most of the asteroids move round the Sun between the paths of Mars and Jupiter.

ATMOSPHERE. The gas round a planet. The Earth's atmosphere is made up chiefly of two gases, oxygen and nitrogen.

AXIS. An imaginary line running through both poles of a planet and also through the centre of its globe.

AURORÆ. Polar lights; bright glows in the Earth's upper air.

BINOCULARS. A pair of telescopes joined together – so that you can use both eyes at once.

COMET. A member of the Sun's family, made up of small pieces of material together with thin gas. A comet lies well outside the Earth's air, and you cannot see it moving quickly across the sky.

CORONA. The very thin gas surrounding the Sun. It is not visible with the naked eye except during a total eclipse of the Sun.

ECLIPSE OF THE MOON. (Lunar Eclipse.) This happens when the Moon passes into the shadow cast by the Earth, so that direct sunlight is cut off from it. A lunar eclipse may be either total or partial.

ECLIPSE OF THE SUN. (Solar Eclipse.) this is due to the Moon passing in front of the Sun, and blotting it out. A solar eclipse may be total (when all the Sun is hidden), partial (when part of the Sun is hidden) or annular (when a ring of the Sun is left showing round the Moon).

EQUATOR. The line running round the Earth which cuts the Earth into two halves, northern and southern.

ESCAPE VELOCITY. The speed at which you would have to go upwards in order to escape from a planet without using any extra power. The escape velocity of the Earth is 11 kilometres per second (40,000 kg per h.).

HYDROGEN. The lightest of all gases. The Sun is made up largely of hydrogen, and water is made up of hydrogen combined with oxygen.

METEOR. A small body which dashes into the Earth's air and burns away.

METEORITE. A larger body, which hits the Earth and may land as a solid lump – perhaps even making a crater.

PLANET. A body with no light of its own, moving round the Sun. There are 9 known planets, of which the Earth is one.

PROMINENCES. Masses of red gas rising from the Sun's surface. With the naked eye, they can be seen only during a total solar eclipse.

SATELLITE. A 'moon' – a body moving round a planet. Our Moon is the only natural satellite of the Earth.

SHOOTING-STAR. The bright streak in the sky caused by the burning-out of a meteor.

SOLAR SYSTEM. The Sun's family. It includes the nine planets, the satellites, the asteroids, comets, meteors and meteorites, as well as the Sun itself.

STAR. A globe of hot gas, shining by its own light. The Sun is a star, and all stars are suns.

SUNSPOT. A darker patch on the surface of the Sun.

TELESCOPE, REFLECTING. A telescope which collects its light by using a curved mirror.

TELESCOPE, REFRACTING. A telescope which collects its light by using a special piece of glass known as a lens (object-glass).

ZODIAC. The belt round the sky in which the Sun, the Moon and the bright planets are always to be found.

TABLE OF THE PLANETS

Planet	Distance from Sun, in kilometres	Time taken to go round the Sun	Diameter kilometres	Number of moons
Mercury	57,600,000	88 days	4,800	0
Venus	107,200,000	$224\frac{3}{4}$ days	12,320	0
Earth	148,800,000	$365\frac{1}{4}$ days	12,682	1
Mars	226,400,000	687 days	6,720	2
Jupiter	772,800,000	$11\frac{3}{4}$ years	141,920	13
Saturn	1,417,600,000	29 years	120,160	10
Uranus	2,852,800,000	84 years	46,880	5
Neptune	4,468,800,000	$164\frac{3}{4}$ years	50,400	2
Pluto	5,865,600,000	248 years	5,900	0

The main asteriods move between the paths of Mars and Jupiter; the largest of them is Ceres, and the brightest is Vesta. Pluto has a strange path which sometimes brings it closer-in to the Sun than Neptune.

THE ASTRONOMY QUIZ BOOK BY PATRICK MOORE 25p

552 54056 0   Carousel Non Fiction

Patrick Moore, well known through television coverage of Apollo moon shots has directed his talent and enthusiasm into translating mysteries of the skies into terms that we can understand. This book is full of fascinating quizzes and is expertly illustrated with easy to follow diagrams.

TOMORROW'S WORLD Vol 2 – THE TOOLS   30p
OF CHANGE BY JAMES BURKE AND RAYMOND BAXTER

552 99583 5   Carousel/Corgi

Based on the BBC T.V. programme, TOMORROW'S WORLD, this book takes a look at some of the latest developments in science and technology. Readers of all ages will find it a fascinating and stimulating book, profusely illustrated with photographs.

ALL ABOUT CRICKET BY BRIAN JOHNSTON   35p

552 54053 6   Carousel Non Fiction

Who better to convey to us the tension and excitement of first class cricket than Brian Johnston. All sport lovers will welcome this edition which is completely revised and up dated by the author.

INDIAN OCEAN TREASURE BY ARTHUR C. CLARKE   30p

552 54049 8   Carousel Non Fiction

Arthur C. Clarke is one of the best known science fiction writers on whose stories the film, 2001 . . . A Space Odyssey, was based. This is a story of a real life treasure hunt and the gripping adventure is well mapped and illustrated.

TALES TOLD BY THE FOSSILS BY CAROLL LANE FENTON
Vol. 1: UNEARTHING LIFE'S PAST   552 54046 3
                                                   30p each
                                        Carousel Non Fiction

This volume explains what fossils are, how they are found and how they divide the earth's history into an orderly series of ages.

Vol. 2: FROM DINOSAURS TO MAN   552 54047 1

Traces the history of life from the late Triassic period, 230 million years ago when lizard-hipped dinosaurs lived, up until 100,000 years ago, when mankind had developed from ape-man to Neanderthal man.

HOKE'S JOKES, CARTOONS AND FUNNY   20p
THINGS BY HELEN HOKE   Carousel Non Fiction

552 54063 3

Every page of this book is packed with colourful cartoons, jokes and riddles.

LOOKING AT HISTORY BY R. J. UNSTEAD   30p per volume

CAVEMAN TO VIKINGS   552 54067 6
THE MIDDLE AGES   552 54068 4
TUDORS AND STUARTS   552 54069 2
QUEEN ANNE TO QUEEN ELIZABETH 11   552 54070 6
                                        Carousel Non Fiction

These four books which have sold over 5 million copies in hardback, provide the ideal way to find out about the past. There are hundreds of illustrations and the text is lively and informative. They are a real Unstead masterpiece.

THE HOW AND WHY WONDER BOOK   35p
OF VOLCANOES

552 86567 2

Volcanoes are one of the awe-inspiring phenomena which bring
both excitement and devastation to man. This book conveys all
these feelings, together with providing excellent historical and
general coverage.

HOW AND WHY WONDER BOOK OF   35p
FAMOUS SCIENTISTS

552 86533 8

Beginning with the question, 'What is a scientist?', the answer is
provided in the lives and work of a series of well-known names
from the history of science. Archimedes, Copernicus, Newton,
Darwin, Pasteur, Madame Curie, and Einstein are just some of the
great figures whose personal lives, and scientific discoveries, are
outlined in this book.

THE HOW AND WHY WONDER BOOK OF   25p
THE SPOILT EARTH

552 86556 7

Pollution is one of the most pressing problems that face the modern
world. THE SPOILT EARTH covers the various forms of pollution that threaten our planet, and indeed our everyday life. Only
by knowing the facts can we learn how to protect the balance of
nature and to build tomorrow's world before it is destroyed.

HOW AND WHY WONDER BOOKS OF OUR EARTH
30p

552 86513 3

Despite Man's venture into outer space, the Planet Earth is still the home of all known peoples. Our Solar System may provide a planet of alternative accommodation, but most of us will continue to live on Earth. We should know as much about our planet home as we can. OUR EARTH explains how it was made and how it is changing all the time. A scientific companion to the Carousel series EVERYDAY LIFE IN PREHISTORIC TIMES.

THE HOW AND WHY WONDER BOOK OF WORLD WAR II
30p

552 86557 5

The second world war is already passing into history, yet it began only just over three decades ago. It is distant and remote for todays teenagers, yet the outcome of that Titanic global struggle has affected – and continues to affect – the lives of us all.

All these books are available at your bookshop or newsagent; or can be ordered direct from the publisher. Just tick the titles you want and fill in the form below.

CAROUSEL BOOKS, Cash Sales Department, P.O. Box 11, Falmouth, Cornwall
Please send cheque or postal order, no currency.
U.K. and Eire send 15p for first book plus 5p per copy for each additional book ordered to a maximum charge of 50p to cover the cost of postage and packing.
Overseas Customers and B.F.P.O. allow 20p for first book and 10p per copy for each additional book.

NAME (Block letters) ....

ADDRESS ....

(JULY 75)...
While every effort is made to keep prices low, it is sometimes necessary to increase prices at short notice. Corgi Books reserve the right to show new retail prices on covers which may differ from those previously advertised in the text or elsewhere.